THE ROAD HOME TO YOU
A SINGER'S JOURNEY FROM EXILE TO GOSPEL

TIM DILLINGER

IMAGINATION FURY ARTS
Nashville, TN

The Road Home to You © 2015, 2016, 2019 by Tim Dillinger

ISBN 978-0-692-37371-2 (HC)
ISBN 978-1-944-19003-3 (PB)

All rights reserved. No part of this book may be used or reproduced in any way without written permission from the author, except in critical articles or reviews. Contact the publisher for permission.

Printed in the United States of America
Cover photography by Matt Muller
Book and cover design by Ray Curenton-Dillinger

Publisher's Cataloging-in-Publication data

Names: Dillinger, Tim, author.
Title: The Road home to you : a singer's journey from exile to gospel / by Tim Dillinger.
Description: Nashville, TN: Imagination Fury Arts, 2016.
Identifiers: ISBN 978-0-692-37371-2 (Hardcover) | 9781944190033 (pbk.) | LCCN 2016917869
Subjects: LCSH Dillinger, Tim. | Dillinger, Tim--Health. | Gay men--United States--Biography. | Church--Holiness. | Singers--Biography. | Self-actualization (Psychology). | Spiritual healing. | BISAC BIOGRAPHY & AUTOBIOGRAPHY / Composers & Musicians | POETRY / General
Classification: LCC ML420 .D565 2016 | DDC 784.5--dc23

Second Edition

IMAGINATION FURY ARTS
Nashville, TN
imaginationfuryarts.com

Dedicated to
High Valley (1945-2013)
for being the ground
&
Whaley Lake
for being a haven

Emily Lucille Harris (1945-2011)
&
Whitney Elizabeth Houston (1963-2012)
for living the song

♛ Table of Contents

Foreword by Elizabeth Cunningham	vii
Introduction	1
1/4/2012: Culminating Death	7
7/18/2010: Singing for My Life	9
2/19/2009: Sorrow	11
9/8/2010: No Hiding Place	12
7/13/2010: The Things We Do Not Say	13
7/21/2010: Flying (A Dream)	17
8/6/2010: Homegoing Realizations	19
9/5/2011: Gospel: An Essay	23
1/15/2011: The Freedom Ride	31
1/20/2011: Retirement	35
3/27/2011: Silence	37
2/5/2011: Be Here Now	39
5/26/2009: For Lady Teena Marie (1956–2010)	40
When You Sing to Me	42
6/4/2011: Detaching and Dying	43
10/10/2011: Meeting the Queen	44
6/13/2011: New Life & Associated Remembrances	47
9/12/2011: Back to Square One	50
5/26/2009: Remembering the Song (San Francisco, California)	52
4/10/2011: My Roots Go Down: Remembering New Covenant Holiness Church	55
10/2/2011: Purrs and Talks	57
10/11/2011: Message from Spirit	59
1/6/2012: The Healer Woman/The Hospital Experience	60
1/12/2012: Recovery Realizations	66
1/15/2012: Freedom Ride: A Year Later	67
1/29/2012: The Road Home	68

2/1/2012: HOLY SPIRIT	70
3/17/2012: FLASHFORWARD	72
2/21/2012: ASSIGNMENT	74
7/26/2012: NEW BEGINNINGS	76
THE BATON	79
4/2/2014: NOW	80
7/2/2013 A REVIEW OF *THE BATON: 1985* BY L. MICHAEL GIPSON	82
ACKNOWLEDGMENTS	86

FOREWORD
BY ELIZABETH CUNNINGHAM

Intimate and original, Tim Dillinger's *The Road Home to You* also stands proudly in the venerable tradition of poetry, song, and gospel witness to the dark night of the soul or in song lyric "the midnight hour." When someone faces himself, his life, his death and chooses to say yes again, to come home again, not just to a place but to the beautiful, heartbreaking condition of being human, he becomes a comforter and companion to everyone he encounters. In this moving work of poetry, picture, story, and song, Tim gives us the gift of his wisdom, his wit, his witness, himself. He reminds us that we have spiritual ancestors, that in our loneliest moments, we are not alone. Thank you, combrogo! I'll see you at home.

. . . feel . . . breathe . . . listen . . .
. . . there is no fear . . .
. . . only consciousness . . .
. . . only a message . . .
. . . can you bear to hear it? . . .

. . . i will not resist . . .
. . . i will comprehend . . .
. . . i will comply . . .
. . . i will do the work . . .
. . . i am waking up . . .
. . . feel the pain . . .
. . . let it talk . . .
. . . lay in it . . .
. . . understand it . . .
. . . then take a step . . .
. . . walk with it . . .
. . . integrate it . . .
. . . soon it will meld . . .

1/27/2012

When I Grow up I want to Be a Singer

Hi, my name is Jim Dillinger. When I grow up I want to be a singer. I know you're probably saying "Ew gross a singer". Actually it isn't that gross.

I want to be a singer because God gave me a voice to sing with and that's why I want to do this.

I think I would be good at this because God gave me a talent and I'm to use it.

To help me become a singer I must practice every day.

The place that Jesus will have in this is through the songs I sing people would come to know God.

Jim Dillinger

🕭 Introduction

I have never known a life without music. My first memory of life, at three years old, is exactly that. Music. Reba Rambo on the radio. Like a flash, my second memory is around the same age seeing Shirley Caesar and Andraé Crouch & The Disciples in concert. Within months, I was singing myself and I never stopped. I was on Christian television for the first time at age seven and after that, my voice took me into a vast array of cultures and experiences, all of which seemed to be accelerating and taking me *someplace*.

I moved to Nashville in 2001 and it became my training ground. The musical landscape was rich: singers and songwriters I'd dreamed of meeting and learning from became a part of my day to day life. I found musicians who became a part of my long-term musical tapestry. Like several of my heroes, I made the decision to not restrict myself to singing gospel music exclusively; instead, I became a part of pioneering Nashville's indie soul scene.

It's hard to believe that not much has changed in the religious community over the course of the past 50 years—particularly in the Bible belt—regarding singers who choose to expand their artistry beyond simply singing about matters of faith. Even in 2004, I was accused of singing "devil's music"—the same accusation hurled at Thomas Dorsey when he was pioneering what became gospel music as well as Sam Cooke, Aretha Franklin and any other artist who has dared to see the thread that ties the worlds together. It was easy to move beyond—simply because the accusation, in my opinion, was ridiculous. I'd had debates with pastors about everything from my nose ring to the length of the praise and worship segment of the service. I had reached my intellectual limit.

Walking away from organized religion gave me the opportunity to finally deal with my sexuality in an unfettered manner. While I'd reconciled it with myself in my late teens, I found that I no longer desired to abide by the respectability politics that so many of my friends in the church world and the gospel music industry did—and continue to live by. I came out, while in production on a gospel album, in 2007. That single action began an unraveling process that was so painful—but was entirely necessary to my evolution.

After almost a decade of making music in Nashville, things were coming to an end. The restrictions of living in the Bible belt made me feel claustrophobic. My first heartbreak had taken my breath away. My longtime manager and I were parting ways. Coming out of the closet had stripped me of the strong, local base of support that my music had garnered. I went from sold out, standing room only performances to begging people to come. It was humiliating and devastating—both emotionally and financially. I couldn't believe that being honest about my orientation (which was constantly being questioned) had alienated so many people. I spent my last six months in Nashville delivering commissary items to inmates in the local jails. I was bereft. Theoretically suicidal. I wrestled with finding reasons to wake up.

I did, however, still have my voice. The thought of a new city—and New York of all places—seemed like an exciting prospect. Friends there were enthusiastic and supportive. They opened their home to me and made their living room my bedroom. My first day in New York felt like something out of a dream. I was at the Apollo Theater watching Nona Hendryx, Sarah Dash, and Patti Labelle (together known as Labelle) performing their first concert together in almost thirty years. A few days later, I was watching Liza at the Palace.

And then real life began.

I struggled to sustain myself. I applied for over 150 jobs and discovered that my corporate experience in Florida and my university experience in Nashville meant absolutely nothing. I finally landed a part-time job doing shipping and receiving at a retail store in a little strip mall in Long Island. When I wasn't working, I spent my time trying to line up gigs. I formed a trio with my roommates and through a series of miraculous events, we performed a string of sold out shows at reputable, small venues

performing at The Triad (2009)

with Susaye Greene at The Duplex (2009)

in the city. We spent the summer touring outside of New York. It was exhilarating. I didn't realize, however, that I was hiding. I remember rehearsing for a gig in Los Angeles and my dear friend Susaye Greene pulled me to the side and said "Don't forget about Tim Dillinger."

Something shifted for me on that tour. When we returned home, I was rushed to the emergency room. My left leg had swollen up like a tree trunk. I was sent to a specialist who immediately diagnosed me with lymphedema. He suggested wearing compression socks when I travelled to help control the swelling. I began Googling lymphedema and started working to find the emotional components that were underneath the condition.

We jumped back into performing in the city. A few months later, I woke up the day after an ecstatic, sold-out show at Don't Tell Mama's with a sore throat. A few hours later, I had a fever. The next day, I could hardly move. My temperature was up to 103. I was back in the emergency room and told that I had had a throat infection. Pharyngitis. It took me two weeks to recover on antibiotics.

I ended up having pharyngitis four times that year—after each performance. In my heart, I felt exhausted with singing. I had sung my heart out. My body was telling me to be quiet. To verbalize that, however, would have been to question my entire identity…the reason I was in New York in the first place. I knew nothing *but* the song. My validation came from my voice, but I was angry at the song. I had been sleeping on a pull-out couch for a year. I had no money. Survival was just too hard. I missed my friends. I felt a million miles away from home.

My roommates and I moved from Long Island to Queens, which then forced me to find another job. I found employment at a photography company in Elmont, a town on the border of Long Island and Queens. From where we lived, my commute could take almost two hours, one way. A fifteen-minute walk to the bus stop, a thirty-minute bus ride to the depot, then another forty-five-minute bus ride to Elmont, then another fifteen-minute walk to work. Just as I began the job, I was physically attacked. I felt unsafe. Frightened. The pressure inside of me was ticking like a time bomb.

On my walk home after work, I would buy a bottle of wine. When I got home, I settled myself in my room with gospel music. Three healthy glasses of wine later, I could sleep in peace, just to begin the routine again the next morning. By November of that year, I dreaded performing. Singing suddenly required effort—something that felt unfamiliar to me. The gift had always been the only thing that came naturally. After our last performance that month, I made the decision to move—*someplace*.

My friend Elizabeth Cunningham, an author who is also a counselor, knew the details of my heart's condition and simultaneously had a home available for rental at High Valley, a property that served as a school for many years, and then as a community (and healing space) for many people in upstate New York. I jumped at the opportunity to move there. High Valley was hidden in the country—far from the noise and energy of New York City that felt like it was electrocuting me every time I left the house.

On December 26, 2010 as I was packing to leave Queens, my musical hero Teena Marie transitioned to the otherworld. When I received the news, the last little bit of the song that remained left me. It was the final blow. In her last interviews, she seemed so tired. I recognized it, because it looked so much like I felt. My roommate and spiritual brother, David, came to my room hours after we'd heard the news and said, "I worry that that's going to be you."

When I left Queens, I swore I'd never sing again. There is a place inside—a wellspring, if you will, that the voice comes from. I was never really aware of that until I entered this particular season. Singing had always been second nature. Accessing that place now felt physically impossible. Nearing it was physically painful. I had been rendered voiceless. I wanted to be mute.

I moved to High Valley on January 15, 2011, knowing that I was going there to heal. I had no idea that my healing would culminate in such a dramatic way and manifest itself so physically through my very body—the valley of the shadow of death.

This book is that story. The writings collected here were written for my two closest friends on the date signatures indicated. They were the only people I felt that I could say anything to. The people I wanted to know what was really going on inside. I was living inside "The Prodigal," a song from the first album I ever fell in love with (*The Prodigal…According to Reba* by Reba Rambo)…a song that I realized I had been living since the day I heard it for the first time when I was three. I was so far from home. And I so wanted to go back.

We've all felt estranged from ourselves. Disconnected from our gifts. Lost from love. Alone in the world. But that's just how you live the song. You must become it. I didn't know *that* when I stood on a Foldger's Coffee can in church at three years old, singing in front of people for the first time. But it is what I signed up for—to allow the song to inhabit me, to consume me, to overshadow me, to have a song even when there is not a stage.

These writings are glimpses of my journey home. Each composition stands on its own. Take your time reading them...let them find the resonant chord inside of you.

Wash your face...then pick up all the pieces...and get yourself on home where you belong. —
from *The Prodigal...According to Reba*, written by Reba Rambo-McGuire and Ron Oates, 1979*

---

* *The Prodigal...According to Reba* by Reba Rambo is an essential album. Originally released in 1979 on Greentree Records, it is no longer in print, but can easily be found on eBay.

CULMINATING DEATH

1/4/2012

i woke up this morning aghast at what i saw
a continuation of what started yesterday
red dots on my hands and arms, spread to my legs and feet
purple welts on my legs as well, purple splotches on my side and back
a green bruise on my arm
canker sores in my mouth, purple spots on my tongue and lips
'i feel pretty'

i sat in my chair just before sunrise
and turned on the clip that has fed me for the past week
my girls in new life reunited for emily's homegoing*
they sang one of their old faithfuls, "in his care"
the lyric has been my bread:
"i will not dread, i will not fear, i'm not alone...my god is here...
my soul is in his care"

i began to weep as i watched
i felt his presence...it's so familiar, but never in a common way
it's a gift i cherish
i'm not even embarrassed by how i look when he shows up: i'm usually crying
he loves my tears. he knows they are all affection
even if they are tinged with a question or two
he takes my face in his hands
"you said yes a long time ago," he whispers
"that has never changed. no matter what you thought.
this is all a part of the plan"

i remembered the thread of *"yes"* throughout my life
laid out in my godmother's floor in my teens, weeping it
doubled over in a revival in myrtle beach, screaming it
we sang it every sunday at *the river* for nine months straight

---

*New Life was a gospel group that was a staple of my childhood. Their long-time tenor, Emily Harris, passed away the week of this entry. The lyric is from their song "In His Care", recorded on their *Bring It To Jesus* album on Tyscot Records. It is available digitally.

my last time leading worship at living word, i was possessed by the yes
and now i know that the yes is completely irreversible
no matter what steps are taken after the yes, everything works together
to bring the yes to completion—to its truest fruition
all things are working

"when your spirit speaks to me...with my whole heart i'll agree...
and my answer will be yes, lord, yes..."

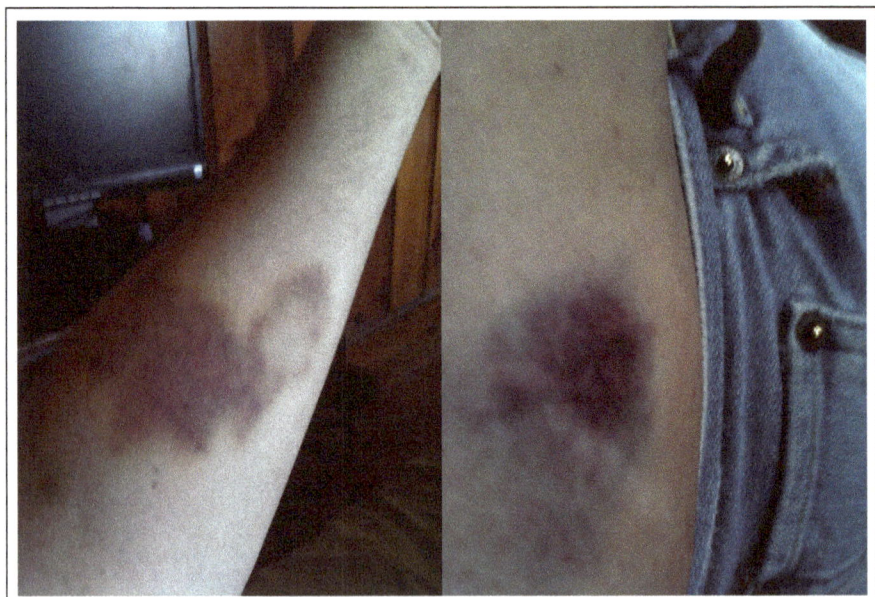

examples of the bruising that made its way across my entire body during this first weekend of January 2012

7/18/2010
SINGING FOR MY LIFE

The Barn at High Valley

a magical night
with the moths and the bats
flowers in my hair
singing to the stars

realizations, stark & beautiful
perhaps we only talk onstage
maybe this is what it is now
the only place we truly see each other: a true soulkiss

cissy houston was in me
angry and determined to sing
to *ex-per-ess*
to jubilee to the high heavens

beautiful secrets i carry to the grave
tapestry weaving: worlds converging
in ways that only a goddess could imagine
thick and thin: the master weaves us in

tears of the touched imprinted
i wish i could sing forever in the barn
barefoot and sweating
without the concern of venues and money and minimums

i wish i never had to leave

i cry in david's arms this am[*]
i don't want to go back to the real world
playing dress up and riding subways
i want to be free

i wonder what the future holds
and how i move forward
when my real self
lives in the lake and emerges to sing

mid-song during "The Barn" concert
photo by Lynn Martin

---
*David Sosa, 1/3 of Soulkiss

SORROW

2/19/2009

my name is sorrow
and there is no consolation for me
i walk a gypsy path
with calluses on my feet
i sing with all i can muster
and give it all for free
i grin, but my name is sorrow
and there is no consolation for me

9/8/2010

NO HIDING PLACE

i want to run to the rocks to hide my face
but dorothy love said there's no hiding place*
every cause for celebration in my life
brings about a cause for lament
i have no idea why, but it's always what happens

i find love, i lose a loved one
a stranger "sees" me, a friend disregards me
it is warm outside, but i am cold
i snuggle in his arms and hear his heart
it reminds me that i am connected

can i just be a hymnsinger?
must i live the song?
what is this way that must be paved?
when obstruction blocks my way
to whom shall i turn?

---

*Dorothy Love Coates, pioneering Gospel artist

THE THINGS WE DO NOT SAY
7/13/2010

silent battles are the worst
psychological warfare
smiling when we want to cry
calming when we want to rage
when we are held hostage
by the things we do not say

i recognize the value
of taking the time to evaluate
but i also maintain
that the heart knows what it knows
it cannot be coerced into being present
the body may be willing
but the spirit certainly isn't

During an argument, a glass was thrown at me. This is the mark it made in the wall. I took the photo to remind myself of what happens "when we are held hostage by the things we do not say."

we spend most of our lives
trying to be loved
enduring things we abhor
from family, friends, lovers, and god
all in the heart of "compromise"
thinking it is give and take

very rarely, however
are we loved on our terms
for our core identity
we dress it up, put makeup on it
and whore it out
until it slowly evaporates
and we wake up one day
wondering where that person went

if home is where the heart is
i'm done interior designing
home's where the heart is
and all of my treasures are there

FLYING (A DREAM)

7/21/2010

"come let's go flying"
he invites with extended hand
as i take his hand, he positions me
in front of him, his right arm around my waist
he raises his left arm and we ascend
effortlessly

in my mind i wonder why this all feels so natural
but it is a question that flashes and doesn't linger
how could it?
with the sensation of wind in my hair, against my face
the tangibility of blue sky and cotton candy clouds
flooding my senses, erasing any thought from the world i know

and then there is his arm
i exhale as it simply holds me as we soar
it is the arm i have waited to feel all my life
i feel myself let go
as i look up over my shoulder
i see his face
confident and strong
this skysoaring thing is normal to him

after touring through the upper regions
we descend to where the people live
we fly over telephone poles
below i can see children playing
cars and buses in the street
i no longer feel like i'm a part of this world
more like i've been to "the real world"
i am now a visitor
oh how i wish they could fly

there are dogs relentlessly barking at us
we pass a reflection from the setting sun
and he holds us in that space
it feels like forever

perfect forever

we land beside an apartment building
i hear teenagers talking on the other side
the traffic sounds have a 3-D effect
he looks at me and without speaking says
"it will take your ears a minute to adjust"

he kisses me
i taste fragrant flowers
two tears stream, one from each eye
"what is your name," i ask
he smiles and says
"you'll see me again"

and disappears in the twinkling of an eye

8/6/2010
HOMEGOING REALIZATIONS

i sang at a homegoing service today
ironic as death has been all over
in various forms all week
i fought to get myself going

i dreaded the arrival of morning
it came and i complied to its request
as i walked to the train station
hot and bothered
i asked god why every step required such effort

luckily i got a seat on the train
i plugged in my earbuds
and nestled into the sounds of gospel
when the storms of life are raging, stand by me

i had a moment of brutal honesty with myself
in an ideal world, i would be a gospel singer
well, let me clarify that: i am a gospel singer
but i am speaking professionally
my inability to lie and not ask questions
make that an impossibility

of course i knew that intellectually
but i don't think i'd ever let myself feel it before
i imagined myself on a field, barefoot
the ground as the truth and i dug my feet into it

it is like being kept away from the one you love
circumstances beyond your control
and you have to work around it
you seek to find an alternate purpose
but there ain't nothing like the real thing

at the homegoing service
i was taken back to the old school days
no musician, we sang congregational songs a capella
finding a beautiful harmony with each other

they called me to sing my solo
i felt the honor of being asked to sing her on home
i felt my teachers around me
i wanted it to be mighty real

long ago, i didn't know nothing about jesus and his love
i had heard about it, but i had never felt it
this manner that comes from above[*]

and me, that fire & holy ghost came together
i was fifteen years old again: pure & unconcerned
loving the song, determined to give it away
letting it touch me first and in turn, the people
this is beauty

i went home, pondering these things in my heart
grateful for the moments i get to be me
wishing they were far more frequent
but regardless, i am a gospel singer

---

*From Dorothy Love Coates' composition "You Must Be Born Again," which I also recorded on my *Gospel* EP. The original version is available digitally, as is mine.

photo by Matt Muller

9/5/2011

♗ Gospel: An Essay

It is the music I heard from the womb. I'm quite certain that my soul heard it long before my body got here. It issued a call and my soul had a response. It is my knee-jerk reaction. Gospel is the music my heart knows.

My mother tells me that she played Andraé Crouch's *Live At Carnegie Hall* while she was pregnant with me and that it is the only album that would put me to sleep at night, after a vigorous dance in my crib. While my first conscious memory of life is hearing Reba Rambo on the radio (the moment and artist that has defined my life), my relationship with gospel music is just as ancient and sacred.

I didn't seek out anything to make that relationship happen...it presented itself through the steps that were natural...the path drew my feet like magnets. They say that it's genetic. I met my father for the first time when I was twenty-four years old and he expressed pieces of his journey to me...and I understood just how determined this call was to express itself through our blood.

My early childhood was shaped by Andraé and The Disciples, The Hawkins Family, Danniebelle Hall, Richard Smallwood, Thomas Whitfield and The Clark Sisters. I would later realize that these were all "contemporary" artists. I knew there was something more. I was drawn to the more "traditional" sounding songs that they did...Danniebelle's "He Leads Us Along," Andrae's take on the congregational song "Can't Nobody Do Me Like Jesus," Tramaine's elongated free-meter reprise of "Going Up Yonder"...I was sniffing for it.

I was a library kid, so I was always combing the shelves...I never knew what I was looking for... but my soul did. I would intuit and I'd know when I'd found what I was there for (a lifelong gift that has also come to define my journey). One day, I found Mark Bego's biography of Aretha Franklin on the shelf. I checked it out and began to read. Names I'd never heard of were jumping out at me: Clara Ward, Dorothy Love Coates and The Gospel Harmonettes, The Davis Sisters, The Caravans. Bego wrote that many of them sang at her father's church; she considered them to be her primary inspirations.

Back in those days, Christian record companies put Buy 4 Get One Free stickers on their albums, so when my grandparents and mother would buy me albums, I'd save the stickers. I would save them and then "special order" things that I wanted that weren't on the shelves, and things that I knew they wouldn't buy for me (crafty, I know).

So I began ordering these gospel legends when I would save up enough stickers.

I lived in Clara Ward's *21 Greatest Hits* (Nashboro Records) in a way that I can't even explain. It was the hymns that I loved. "Beams of Heaven," "The Last Mile of the Way," "I Love the Name Jesus." She also did up-tempo versions of songs that we sang in my grandfather's church, like "When We All Get to Heaven," but we sounded nothing like this when we sang.

The Davis Sisters, The Caravans (and each of them as solo artists), Dorothy Love Coates and The Gospel Harmonettes all became a part of my daily life. One might think I was too young to resonate with such world-weary music, but I wasn't. I felt every note. Related all too well. I began to wear their influence.

In my early teens, I entered a Gospel contest at our local Christian bookstore. I sang an old Thomas Dorsey song, "Search Me Lord." I was inundated with requests to sing at local churches after that. As I started going to these churches to sing, I learned that the trend was that they were all "black" churches. Each church led to another and soon this is how my Fridays, Saturdays, and Sundays were spent. My mother (and often her best friend Valerie) would drive me to sing.

One night, we pulled up to 1625 6th Avenue South in St. Petersburg, Florida, at a little church called New Covenant Holiness Church. That night redefined my life, my path, and my purpose. I didn't know that then, of course. I just knew it was where I was supposed to be, where I belonged, and I was willing to be there by any means necessary.

New Covenant Holiness Church

Theme: Christian MEN and WOMEN working together in unity!

DUAL DAY CELEBRATION
Sovenir Book

1625 6th Avenue South
Saint Petersburg, Florida 33712
(813) 821-3561

Rev. Abraham Dancil, Pastor ASG (a SERVANT of GOD)

In the beginning, I would go to my grandparent's church on Sunday morning. I would fulfill my responsibility (sing), sneak out, and have friends who drove meet me outside. They would drive me to New Covenant and drop me off. I was young (fourteen): so naïve and so completely certain. I knew that someone would take me home. I never even thought about it.

My friends would drop me off on the corner (always making sure to comment about my safety, which was, again, never a concern on my end). You could hear the commotion from New Covenant all the way on the street. I would run from the corner to the church steps, so frightened that I might be missing something. By the time I got there, the pews were already full and I would have to sit on a folding chair.

New Covenant was a small church. Without the folding chairs, it could probably hold eighty people, max. With chairs, it was almost impossible to move. Our pastor's daughter, Linda Sesler, was a powerhouse, charismatic, a dynamo. A preacher first, but could also sing, an evangelist or revivalist at heart. No one could exhort like her. She was conscious of everything happening in the room.

Early in my excursions to New Covenant, I remember making my way in while things were already at fever pitch. Sister Linda was telling the people to raise their hands and tell God *"thank you!"* The first time wasn't enough apparently and she had to drive the point home. As I was settling myself in my seat, she said *"Raise your chocolate..."*—and then she looked at me—*"and vanilla hands...and tell God thank you!"*

While I had never been in services like this in my grandparent's church, everything about this experience was a remembering. Not only did it feel natural, but it was as if some lifelong thirst or drought was being quenched. Like something had been sitting so stuffed down inside of me that now it was rising to the top and it was unstoppable.

I emoted, expressed, and praised like they did. I talked like they did, sang like they did. I was home and I knew it. Within the year, I was living with Mother Morgan and her family, remembering more and more. Mother Morgan was a singer's singer. She had a group and I was an immediate part of it.

"You're old," she would say to me. *"You love those old songs. You're an old soul."*

with Mother Morgan

NEW COVENANT ADULT CHOIR
PSALM 66   PRESIDENT - REV. JOHNNY NOLTON

MAKE A JOYFUL NOISE UNTO GOD, SING FORTHE THE HONOUR OF HIS
ALL YE LANDS;   NAME;
                               MAKE HIS PRAISE GLORIOUS.

circa 1994

We would sing over plates of chitlins and cornbread and our favorite Kiwi Strawberry Mystic soda. While her favorite singers were Mavis Staples and Shirley Caesar, she found great delight in how much I loved Dorothy Norwood and Albertina Walker, in particular.

And we would revive many of those songs as we sang not only in New Covenant, but churches all over the Tampa Bay that would call her to come sing. Soon they were saying *"bring the white boy with you when you come."* And we would show up singing Margaret Douroux's "If It Had Not Been for the Lord (On My Side)," Dorothy Love Coates's "Lord You've Been Good to Me," or Shirley Caesar's "Yes Lord, Yes."

We developed that unique, family harmony that only comes from deep, soulful love and spending nearly every waking moment together. We would sit around the dining room table and play with songs. We prayed together, cooked together, cried and laughed.

Sometimes I would lead testimony service. Sometimes by myself, sometimes with Kenneth and Verinda Jackson, two more singers of the highest order. In testimony service, anyone could stand up and sing. It was in these services that the greatest, unpublished songbooks of all time were opened up. People sang songs that their great-grandparents sang: old field hollers, simple three-word call-and-response songs, hymns. My godmother, Mother Morgan, was a pro at pulling out a song people hadn't sung in thirty or forty years and turning the church inside out.

Sometimes we had a full band, sometimes we had no musicians at all. We had our hands; they became an entire percussion kit. We had washboards and tambourines, and , of course, we had our voices. It was a living, breathing expression of handmade art.

When we sang in those services, we were, essentially, buck naked. We bared it all. It was raw, it was ragged, sometimes bloody, and the most beautiful thing I have ever seen. When we would expose ourselves, the congregants met us in that place. Their experience merged with ours. The unspoken took tangible shape, Sometimes it wasn't even a song, but a testimony, a groan, a moan, words that could not be uttered but they could be felt. The spirit of agreement. It was always a "Yes" that brought us together. Our own personal OM.

We were not dignified. I've seen people in full Holy Ghost takeover remove dentures, hair, hats, or anything else that might impede their ability to let go and let God. I've seen snot, sweat, and fingernails fly when the Spirit takes over. We would all become resident nursemaids for each other, swarming with tissue, paper towels, lapcloths, and hugs when so needed.

I had incredible experiences in "the mist," as I called it sometimes. It was the first conscious lesson I ever had of knowing how to be in the moment. My godmother would exhort, sometimes while making the announcements, *"I want you to think... [insert dramatic pause]...of his goodness."* And we would. We would think of whatever that meant for us, and that would invoke us. I would often find myself doubled over, unleashing loud wailing Indian war whoops, tears flowing, enraptured in recognition of all of the blessings in my life. It still happens in the privacy of my home.

Don't let my summary of our attributes steer you wrong: we had issues too. All of the typical church drama existed. There was in-fighting and power plays. Hurtful words were exchanged from time to time. But this was my life for a decade, and the lessons that I gleaned in that tiny church and all of the places that it took me, brought out so many buried treasures that were just sitting inside of me waiting to be mined.

The next decade of my life took me on another adventure, but the gospel was always present with me. I still find myself firmly rooted in my gospel past. I feel it becoming more and more visible and commanding in my life than ever.

No matter how it is couched and expressed today, Gospel music is not theology. It is not dogma. It is personal experience. It is the blues, it is joy and pain, the recognition of our exhaustion and our hope for a better day. Gospel music is far more than a song or a voice or a church. Gospel music is about the convergence of a song, a personal experience and a voice willing to move beyond their own consciousness in telling the story.

I fully believe in the power of our confession. But I also believe there is great necessity in acknowledging our present, our emotions, our fears, our discontent, our worry, for only in that acknowledgement does hope have the most succulent scent. People have turned their backs on many of these great songs because they do not necessarily contain a "positive confession" in this life, albeit heaven is always promised. But I maintain that, despite our confession, life does not always promise us our desired outcome: dreams do not always come true, no matter how much we may believe for them. There is, however, always another plan...and God's or not, sometimes we have to gear ourselves up to live through it, and lament the one that we lost.

Beams of heaven as I go / through this wilderness below / Guide my feet Lord in peaceful ways / Turn my midnights into day / When in the darkness I should grope / Faith always sees a star of hope / And soon from all of life's griefs and dangers / I shall be free someday
But I do not know how long it will be / Nor what the future holds for me / But this one thing I know / Lord if you lead me / I'm going on home someday —
from "Beams of Heaven" by Charles Albert Tindley (1851–1933)

THE FREEDOM RIDE
1/15/2011

there's nothing left for me here.
nothing at all.

i stood in the kitchen one last time
hugging neema, the hairless sphinx, who belonged to one of my roommates
the cat who licked my tears one frightening night
whose love i would not have survived the past two years without

perhaps that moment in the kitchen
was the first time i ever truly felt why people stay:
stay in things they know are not good for them...
because there is some bizarre comfort in familiarity

and then i remembered...
the screaming, the terror, the shoe that hit my face
being dragged across the bed, the blood on my leg
my surrender to the blows, the numbness afterwards

i've got to go neema. i'm sorry.
the tears fell. i was heaving.
hands shaking, legs like jello
when i opened the door, the cold air chilled my bones

i didn't think i'd ever get that 10 foot truck out of the driveway
it took me about 45 minutes
it was everything i hate about new york in one polarizing moment
perhaps indicative of my own contradictory resistance to this essential change

when i finally did get out of the driveway
ihe few blocks to the van wyck expressway felt like forever
it was as if i was in a car chase in an action flick
go. go. go. the voice inside screamed. *get out of here.*

and i couldn't go fast enough.

it wasn't until i got out of the city's madness
that i felt the anxiety subsiding
elizabeth had given me instructions not mapquestable
to provide me a ride with more beauty & less interstate

one of my roommates gave me their yorkie, moja
moja demanded to go with me
take.me.with.you., i heard her say from her crate one day
i ignored her.
she said it one more time a few hours later and i conceded
i looked over at her, wearing her little winter jacket
sleeping as if she hadn't slept in years
i held her paw and cried again
i had really gotten away. i couldn't believe it.

all kinds of memories replayed as i drove

iris the busdriver, who i met one night riding the bus home to queens
iris: *where you headed?*
me: *south richmond hill, ma'am*
iris: *ma'am?? where you from, boy?*
me: *nashville*
iris: *well, you won't make it long here. you're too nice.*

and then there were the venues
the pretentiousness of the owners
the fighting to get booked in the first place
and then ultimately, the thieving they do at the door when you shock them and sell out

and then...

the musicians who don't rehearse
the product you don't sell
the moment you realize someone only cares for you because of your gift

the look in someone's eyes when they are seduced by the prospect of fame

the part-time job that pays $8 an hour
the screaming boss you endure
the $100 a month you pay to get to the job
the food stamps you couldn't live without

the sores on your back from sleeping on a pull-out couch for a year too long
the basement flood that destroyed your only possessions
the glass that flies across the room when you say the wrong thing
the misconception that fighting is synonymous with love

the avoidance of eye contact on the subway
the uncomfortable groping when the bus is too full
the sounds that make you feel shell shocked
the bottle of wine that gets you to sleep at night

the objectification of your body
the weariness that comes from chanting
the price you pay
...to live the song and give it all for free

don't let them kill you the way they killed me
one of my recently departed teachers said to me in a dream
rest. be quiet. don't sing until you want to
and if you don't ever want to sing again...don't!

as i passed that familiar right turn off of the clinton corners exit from the taconic
something in my soul let go. this is a new beginning.
i exhaled. i cried again.
moja stretched and sat up for the first time this entire trip

i drove the narrow road on sunset trail
minutes away from this new home
on the land that has been my safe place
since the beginning of my time in new york

providence

i have no idea what i'm going to do here
who i'm going to be
or where this is taking me
maybe i'll be here forever and maybe i never have to be anyone again
i welcome that

Sunset Trail, Clinton Corners, NY

RETIREMENT

1/20/2011

if i tilt my chair in the living room
i can sit facing the sun
beaming through a tall window
it shines through trees
with icicled branches
that i can hear applaud...
if i turn down the davis sisters

i stood in the center of what felt like a circle
as i walked the dog this am
the cold wind hit my face
i closed my eyes
and was thankful for my new home

my boss & i worked from her house yesterday
on the way back to my house
she pronounced, *"you don't have to worry about dying young this time"*
out of nowhere, shocking me and her
my body chilled as i cried
as she verbalized something i had felt, but never said

i had dinner with my neighbor-friend, debbie
we sipped red wine and played old 10-inch records
acoustic blues, big band, and early rock-n-roll
over a fresh veggie combo plate
and word games afterwards
i walked home in the moonlight

a friend emails and congratulates me on my retirement
that's really what it is. i just hadn't used that word
i feel my insides relaxing
i am making this house my home, brick by brick
this dog and i

my neighbor-friend, Debbie   my beloved yorkie, Moja

3/27/2011

SILENCE
(IN MEMORY OF LOLEATTA HOLLOWAY 11/5/1946–3/21/2011)

the room is illuminated with light
it gives the false appearance of warmth
i step outside
and it is chilly
but i sit in my living room and love the light

these days i find my joy in silence
my own silence that is
loleatta holloway's voice sings to me
i don't sing along; i merely listen
only you can brighten my day

we had a singing supper last night
i sang along the first few songs
then i just couldn't anymore: just couldn't
i wanted to simply listen
have i lost my song?

elizabeth and cait gently prod me to sing
i oblige, only out of love for my companions
i teach them a congregational song
"i know i've been changed"
i hear the change in my voice
it is lower, it is gravelly, it is world-weary.

i listen to heaven songs
tramaine's "going up yonder" dissolves me
the emotional unearthing of the past week
makes heaven sound quite serene
but this is temporary. i know that.

i remember a night, three years ago
in the midst of a heart-break experience,
while reading *the passion of mary magdalen*[*]
a book I'd found so accidentally on a library shelf
a voice asked me *"would you like to die tonight?*
you can close your eyes and just go to sleep
if that's what you want"

the passion had given me a reason to wake up
i had to keep reading: i was captivated by maeve and esus
i told the voice that i wanted to live
and i can't lie: i have doubted my answer numerous times
but i'm here: finding my way: walking the stony path

my boss & i had a conversation about faith
we discuss the rapture and he asks if i believe in a second coming
i tell him that i think it's representative of a consciousness shift
no trumpets, no flying, no escape plan
this is life: live it

i remind him of maeve's country of life:
it's hard, she said, but she celebrated that stony path
it's ugly, it's beautiful, it's complicated, it's carefree
it's what it is, i tell him
he cries

so my song has changed
not necessarily sung, but spoken
it's conversation: its rhythm is a primal heartbeat
no stages, no cover charge, no merch to push
it is in the moment: can you feel it?

---

[*] *The Passion of Mary Magdalen* by Elizabeth Cunningham (Monkfish Book Publishing) is a fictionalized re-write of the Jesus story. It is undoubtedly one of the most amazing books I've ever read.

BE HERE NOW
2/5/2011

i am inside
and i am content
the walls are velvet
the silence is golden
i am nested

contentment smells like cornbread
and the butter melts on top
i have no need to leave
there is no other place i need to be
but here. now.

i am inside
i sleep for what feels like years
i wake up and expect my hair to be white
i ran for forever & a day
and now that i'm here, i don't ever want to leave this place

i have spent my life singing
the song brought me here
and now i relish the silence
life in my living room: ah, the irony
i am inside: inside myself

FOR LADY TEENA MARIE (1956–2010)
5/26/2009

she is a whirl: a white light
spirit blurs the picture
i see a funnel rising within her
it rises out of her and she spins within it
swirling glory majesty
she is carried up on her throne

the goddess lives
and is anointing the people
those with ears to hear
hear what the spirit says
and we drink of the cup
baptized by flames
we revel in the glory of this sweet black rain

she is a channel
a vessel willing to be poured through
i can feel this for sure
a shaman
a priestess
a healer
ordained by the rose
part of a holy bloodline
and her name is
ivory

taken during a memorial ritual for Lady on December 26, 2011, a year to the day of her passing

WHEN YOU SING TO ME
(Originally written for *The Baton: 1985*, unreleased)

i rest in the secret place
a feathered wall of sound
your voice is surrounding me
serenity is found
it unearths the hidden memories
sacred, holy ground
settles & consoles me
i submerge, but never drown

when you sing to me
the song is my reality
when you sing to me
i climb the summit fearlessly
when you sing to me
the otherworld i plainly see
when you sing to me
i am...i am...complete

you fill empty rooms
with melodies, ten feet tall
enveloping, changing power
inside the dewdrops fall
you take me distant places
invite me to the ball
sweet as the georgia rain
you give your all and all

when you sing to me
i live where earth & heaven kiss
when you sing to me
the motherland, eternal bliss
when you sing to me
all that wasn't finally is
when you sing to me
i am...i am...complete

singer
your melody sets captives free
singer
the lushest, richest rhapsody
singer
you are the song inside of me
singer
you are eternity

6/4/2011

DETACHING AND DYING

we all have bursts of energy
concentrated times that we create
seemingly as steamrollers
when it's over, it's over
we feel lost afterwards...
where is the adrenalin...
the drive...
the movement...
we wonder what is next...
we seek direction...

creativity changing forms is frightening...
we are told that *"this"* (whatever "this" is)
is what we do...who we are...
then when that identity—the mask—falls away
we see a face that is unfamiliar
we must look into the fine lines on our face
and acknowledge the people who put them there
acknowledge our own worries and fears that we now wear

i talked to an eighty-seven-year-old man this week
who just completed a book of spiritual principles
he considers it his life's work...
he told me he had no aspiration to reach ninety
that the completion of this work was the end for him
that he was done

i don't think i am approaching physical death
but i do understand the feeling of detachment
from all that has defined me
to become more and more formless with every shape-shifting
questioning myself less and less
moving into my stream of life with little to no resistance
knowing that i can ride the waves to whatever my destination is

MEETING THE QUEEN

10/10/2011

my morning started off discombobulated

i had an early morning car appointment
i went to bed early precisely because of it
i woke up at 4
and had no idea why i was up so early

i made coffee
i fed my animals, i read, i made breakfast
i took another nap
got ready for work...got halfway there
and remembered. *what. the. hell.*

i was, however, ultra excited about today
"the queen," caroline muir—the tantra goddess was visiting[*]
she's here for a workshop and wanted to come meet us
her ex-husband charles deemed her "the queen" early in their marriage
and she entirely lives up to her title—via skype & emails

meeting her in the flesh was all of that and more

she came to the office with one of her hosts
she hugged paul[**] regally
turned to me and her beautiful green eyes met mine
"oh what biiiiiiiiiig heart energy you have" she purred

i have five cats. i know a purr when i hear one.

we hugged and spontaneously began to cry
it was the holy ghost. warm and gooey. the river was flowing

[*]Caroline Muir is a renowned healer and teacher. She and her ex-husband Charles Muir helped spread the message of Tantra across North America in the 1980s. Caroline continues her work today and published her memoir, *Tantra Goddess* (Monkfish Book Publishing) in 2011.

[**]Paul was my employer at the time.

i felt her big heart against my chest.
we released each other and just looked into each other's eyes
"you are angelic," she declared

"as are you, queen…as are you," i replied

paul and caroline's friend mary were watching in wonderment
we sat down and had soulful conversation about her book
about sexuality and spirituality—the blend & the convergence of the two,
the book publishing industry, and contemplated her future
we decided that lunch was in order.

caroline and i held hands and walked to the restaurant.

the restaurant felt incredibly loud
everyone in rhinebeck was off for columbus day
tourists were trudging through and children were present
for hearing purposes, paul & mary drifted into their own conversation
leaving caroline and me to our own devices

we talked about "the work"
work that is foreign to me on one level, but somehow familiar to me on another
we talked about the healing energy in our hands—the heat
the fire of the stars, as elizabeth called it in her novels
the holy ghost, as we called it in church

i remembered and shared the story of an ex
how one kiss elicited a weeping fit that lasted for an hour
an unstoppable, uncontrollable river of tears that embarrassed him
he felt my hands, hot and red; my face flushed and warm
"what did you do to me," he asked; half frightened, half grateful

the few people i've shared that kind of intimacy with
have all had that experience
it frightened them and puzzled me
but reading caroline's book helped give me a context
while there is a spiritual component to those experiences

there's also the plain & simple reality of what happens
when we truly take the time to see people
really see them

it's the choice of just singing the song
or living it

paul & mary caught the end of our conversation
mary commented with a big smile
"these two really have something happening with each other"

i looked into her eyes
it was as if i were sitting inside of her soul
they were green...but suddenly they were almost translucent
grey...melding with the white
one of the most beautiful things i've ever seen

another hour passed
we brainstormed more & dreamed aloud
we held hands as we walked back to the office
she autographed some galleys for some bloggers who will be interviewing her

our time was up & it was bittersweet
we embraced for what felt like minutes
our eyes were glassy again
we promised that it would not be our only meeting
i know that i made a friend for life

it was the experience i needed today. in this moment.
after last week, which felt like it was hand delivered from hell.
"you have the mojo," paul whispered when she left
*"those are the kinds of women i come from, paul...
...they are my kin...that wasn't work...that was home..."*

6/13/2011

NEW LIFE & ASSOCIATED REMEMBRANCES

L to R: Francine Belcher, Nuana Dunlap, Angela Wright-Primm, Emily Harris, Beverly Crawford (in front)

a nashville friend surprised me today with a dvd transfer
of bobby jones and new life's *"bring it to jesus"* concert
i've been working on an essay about these women
for almost two years now...
then in the emotional catharsis of my move here
finally had the wherewithal to sit and watch the old videos i had
of these women who were such a part of me
i would watch them on television every week
and they would firedance
i wanted to get in the fire with them

i was so drawn that i flew myself to nashville
a month after graduating from high school to see them
one of them and her husband took to me

and we would do revivals together every time they came to florida
i would drive all over the state to meet them
and everything i learned in our little holiness church
was only amplified by my times with her

she knew how to start a fire with jugs of water
in entirely uninspired and unimpressed churches
and when the church was already on fire
she knew how to blow that micki-ficki wide open
i would watch in wonder
she would pull me out and make me start them too
other times, when the fire was in full throttle
we would dance together

years later when i actually moved to nashville
—after new life had long broken up—
one of the other girls took me under her wing

we would get together through the week
pray in her garage, write and record songs
and do occasional services together
through her i met another of the girls
who would nickname me "sunshine"

my life has taken a million turns since those days
as i've been in my time of sabbatical
i see all of the worlds that i have woven in and out of
i love each of them equally
but in my quest to live an honest life
my search for information…knowledge
has taken me into new worlds…
worlds that seem to be disapproved of by my old ones
while i live in the mystery wholeheartedly
i do believe there are things that we know
but are afraid to say, for fear of being misunderstood
in that we rob ourselves of our truth
if only we could tear down these walls

i see how the worlds all work together
how they are all a part of each other
how people miss the beauty that lies in there
saddens me

maybe that's why i cry uncontrollably
when i watch these videos
i can't help myself
it's innate in me
because i remember…remember…remember…
i know what i know

i remember seeing instantaneous healing
when new life took over tennessee performing arts center
and for three hours no one sang
no one could bring us under control
we roared in unexpected, spontaneous ecstasy
the holy ghost and mama africa took over
we heard drums that weren't there
we remembered, we turned ourselves over
all we knew to do was surrender
to what our bodies knew from many moons ago

it was all real

i know i didn't see these things to hoard them
or to simply ponder them in my heart
but when i think about telling the stories
a part of me wants to tuck them in my bosom
and embrace them as mine alone
i know they are sacred
i worry about whether others will see them as such
i don't want them to be laughed at
i want them to be seen…heard…felt…

let the way be opened

BACK TO SQUARE ONE
9/12/2011

there are no accidents
every single incident in our lives
is working to create one amazing
revelation
if we're only willing to listen

last week i was so heavy
i-want-to-die kind of heavy
every step felt like it weighed 100 pounds
i was short, snappy, and cantankerous
over it

i drove to work on edge

beverly crawford squalled all the way in
"holy ghost, we need to hear from you"
i felt like i hit the ground running when i got to the office
but my ears were open

i heard a voice say *"go back to square one...start all the way over"*

this weekend the movie in my mind replayed
every single time i gave my power to someone
i've been doing it since i was a teenager
it was painful to watch again...why did i do that?

square 1
i know what that means
and i'm going to be about the business of going back there
making the decisions i wish i'd made
i get a chance to make them now
for the first time, i can see clearly

there is no fear here
severe exhaustion perhaps, but no fear
i have moments of exhilaration, moments of dread
but i am climbing each mountain
trying to find my song again

REMEMBERING THE SONG
(SAN FRANCISCO, CALIFORNIA)

5/26/2009

i spent the afternoon
in the music room
of a dear friend
talking gospel
reliving the history

the walls were adorned with the legends
clara ward, james cleveland
marion williams, the caravans
i sat on the floor like a kid again
sifting through her vinyl collection
and we dished, as gospel singers do

she turned on the keyboard
and we went way back
the davis sisters, dorothy love coates…
the most current we got
was andraé crouch and danniebelle hall

as we sang these old songs
"twelve gates to the city"
"lord keep me day by day"
i felt like i was back at the dining room table
with my godmother back in florida
singing harmony
and establishing the family bond

i felt joy
unabashed joy
for the first time in awhile
as i felt like i was holding the song
—or these songs—
so close to me

i cradled them, i kissed them
i loved them
and when we were done
i felt a little tinge of the sadness i feel
when a show is over
but instead of missing someone
i was missing the song

with The Clara Ward Singers at the Apollo Theater (2008)

New Covenant Holiness Church, St. Petersburg, FL

MY ROOTS GO DOWN: REMEMBERING NEW COVENANT HOLINESS CHURCH

4/10/2011

it was like stepping into the frying pan
the kind that has an array of peppers
yellow, red, green: all together
jalapeno and a pinch of habanero
onions, garlic, seasoning salt
and whatever other component comes to mind
to make a rich, spicy plate

we would gather every sunday
dressed to the nines (even me)
not for form or fashion of course:
and that really is the truth
when the spirit would fall
hats, heels, hair, false teeth
or whatever else might hinder
would quickly be cast aside: and gladly

let go, let god was our mantra
we had no schedule
no rules either, really
we had an understanding: a feeling between us
we knew how to see whose turn it was
(juanita bynum would say years later
"it might not be your time on the program, but it's your time in the spirit")
we could look at each other and know
we knew how to undergird and support that person and push them forward
go 'head, go ' head

one sunday, i was unexpectedly called for a solo
i started singing "he looked beyond my fault & saw my need", a favorite from my childhood
half-through the first chorus, i felt it all shift

i closed my eyes: i wanted to feel it, not see it

i felt myself being carried.
i was high above the ground
i felt hands underneath me, supporting me
all i had to do was sing
i didn't even have to hold myself up

i had finished the song, but i heard myself in a preach
"he looked," i shouted
"he looked," they responded
i heard my godbrother screaming
it was primal: gut-level
my godmother yelled from her seat *"build it up!"*

i opened my eyes
and saw spiritual pandemonium
they had met me in that place
a place of gratitude for the power
that supplies for us despite all that we do not know
or rather, all that we do not remember
he looked

someone was running
someone else was doubled over
we should have had a vial to collect the tears
one of my brothers started dancing
and we all met *him* there
someone linked their arm in his and danced with him

my roots go down
this is where i come from
so on sunday mornings in particular, i honor that
even though i think those years
more than bleed their way through on a daily basis
they are woven intricately into my tapestry

PURRS AND TALKS
10/2/2011

i woke up saturday morning to an email from my birth mother
telling me that my grandmother had died in the night
in the moment, i felt nothing
blank. it was like reading an email that said "penis enlargement: click here"

i drove into town and as i headed back home
it started to sink in
i remembered that silent wish that i'd felt through my entire childhood
when she would dress me in her clothes and threaten me with hell afterwards
"god, i wish she would just die"

that wish somehow held on in my body
even after i left home as a teenager
and even after i'd left florida in 2001 and cut communication
as i drove back to the house
i felt my body releasing the feeling i'd been holding for most of my life

when i got home, i started a load of laundry and came upstairs
sleep overtook me. i woke up four hours later
my body felt almost fluid
i rented a movie on itunes
and fell asleep again within minutes

i woke up to a glass that the cats broke at 5 am
i did my morning rituals, made the coffee
and turned on the bob dylan documentary i'd rented
and got transported in time
his poetry, his thoughts, his freedom, his adventure finding home

the realization that i will return to my city hit me this week
the realization that this is not forever has actually been a relief
the button turned on this week. i felt it. i miss and love nashville
of course, i know no timing, but i will go home. for good

it gives me the best butterflies

as soon as bob dylan ended, the sleep took me over again
this time i heard a voice ask me to let myself go
i did
i felt myself falling. at warp speed. without fear.
i knew there was no bottom

the next thing i knew i was flying
through these energy spirals that were directing me
i had to make no decisions or think about where i was going
the spirals were like magnets, pulling me at warp speed
exactly where i was supposed to go
i woke up underneath all five cats and with moja sleeping on my neck
my new favorite sound is their simultaneous purring when they're sleeping
it's like being in the middle of vibrating harmony
there is absolutely nothing like it
nothing.

mama said i'm on a healing adventure
and i can't think of another way to say it
that really sums it up
i'm in the center of the center of the middle of it
i'm savoring the sleep, the dreams, the realizations, the purrs and the talks

with one of my kittens, Shug Avery

From: "David Sosa"
To: "Tim Dillinger"
Subject: Message from Spirit

OCTOBER 11, 2011

Oh your weary soles...how they do ache. The spurs of your heels, the curve of your toes, the arch of your feet that already know the tough road they walk barefoot. You walk the hard road no one wants to acknowledge. You walked this path many lifetimes before. Of course your feet are tired. Must angels always fly when they have two good feet? Their mission doesn't change...their gifts do not change... but they are sent here to do what they do in the only way they know how to do it: letting God work through them. Like most jobs, they don't have to like it and they may not even have to get it, but they still have to do it. You will walk until your feet are worn...until your socks come away at the seams. You will walk until the jagged rocks on that road you walk shed some of your blood, but where those drops stain, life, inspiration, encouragement will grow. Who said your job is for you? Who said your job might bring some sense of self-satisfaction? It is never that easy.

You teach, you share, you minister, you heal, you comfort and you entertain. At the end of the day you realize your feet still hurt. No rest comes now, because you are walking in your right path. Soon your bare feet will touch the soft grass of the place that calls to you. The land will once again reconnect with you and the vines and leafy foliage will wrap around you in that moment and secure you in place, and you will become a still monument. No need to walk or move, your work is done, your journey ended, your feet found home. Rest is your accomplishment, your restitution for the many lives you have touched and the walking you have done in paths others may now dare to walk.

My spirit says you are resonating more and more with "going home" songs...more than usual. You need to do cleanings and meditate again. Yes, you are old and tired...weary. The women you are resonating with left the world tired and sick. You are telling their story and the illumination of your intent is attracting them closer to you. You've got to lift them up. Light a candle for them, they are influencing you. They are telling me it's harder and harder for you to just get out of bed despite your love of the land you live on and the kitties, it's just barely enough. Give them light, visually and in your intention. You still have things to do and you can't join them just yet.

THE HEALER WOMAN/THE HOSPITAL EXPERIENCE

1/6/2012

a healer woman called to check on me
and announced that she was coming to "work on me"
she enters my room with such confidence
carrying drums, tuning forks, and singing bowls

i chuckled to myself wondering what the doctors and nurses must think

when they started transfusing me
lynn and marion were doing reiki on me
i've been playing gospel on my laptop since then
and now this

as she settles, she pulls out a bowl of popcorn
popped with olive oil and seasoned with garlic
my taste buds danced
a relief after a week of putrid hospital food

her hair is the color of my beloved yorkie, moja
we've joked several times that moja loves her
because moja thinks they are related
even though she seems much more catlike in spirit

she began to speak...

"we have to acknowledge how close you were to death
what happened to you happened because you have been living an incongruent life
what is in your heart isn't what you're living
you've settled for something that your soul doesn't want"

and then i cried

the voice i'd heard in my living room the prior weekend hadn't stopped playing over and over

"what you're getting ready to experience is going to take you home…
you said yes a long time ago…and this experience is a direct result of your yes…
you have nothing to dread, nothing to fear…you are not alone
this experience is going to take you home"

the tears were now flowing full force
she took out a singing bowl and hit it softly with the striker
i closed my eyes and went into the sound
it began to carry me: past the discomfort, past the pain

suddenly i was in a circle, surrounded by faces i so love
my teachers. my heartbeats.
isn't it amazing how people you've never met can come to mean so much?
they had transitioned in recent years and with them, a part of me died

the loss of their physical form felt so great
i was bereft when they left the earth
so bereft that i abandoned the gift that had lived in me
since my earliest memory of life

i wept in their presence
one, who passed at a mere fifty-four years of age, had returned to the appearance
she had in her thirties
another, who had been given the moniker of queen in her earth-days,
looked exactly the same as when she left—girded in her power, feistiness, and heart
she was in the center of the circle
i was seated in the heart of the circle, with them surrounding me

"we're happy you chose to stay," she spoke
eye to eye, we were locked into each other
"you could have left—and nobody would have judged you for it
it would have been all right."

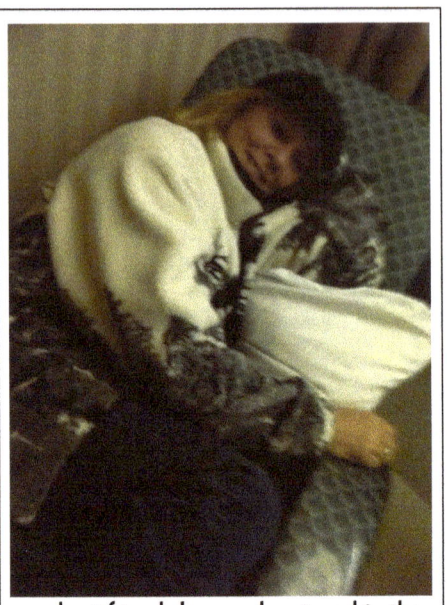
my best friend, Lynn, who stayed in the hospital with me every night

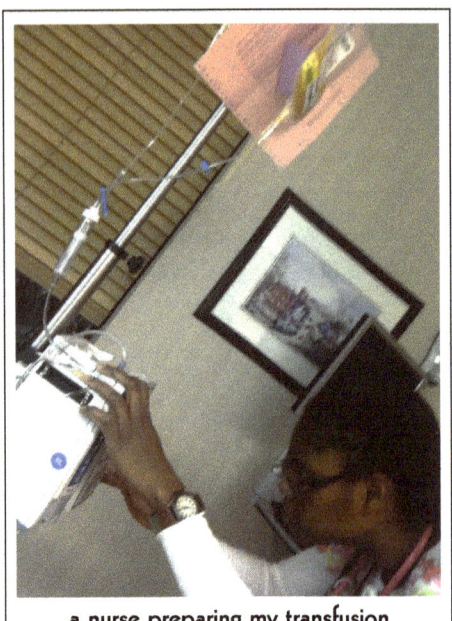
a nurse preparing my transfusion

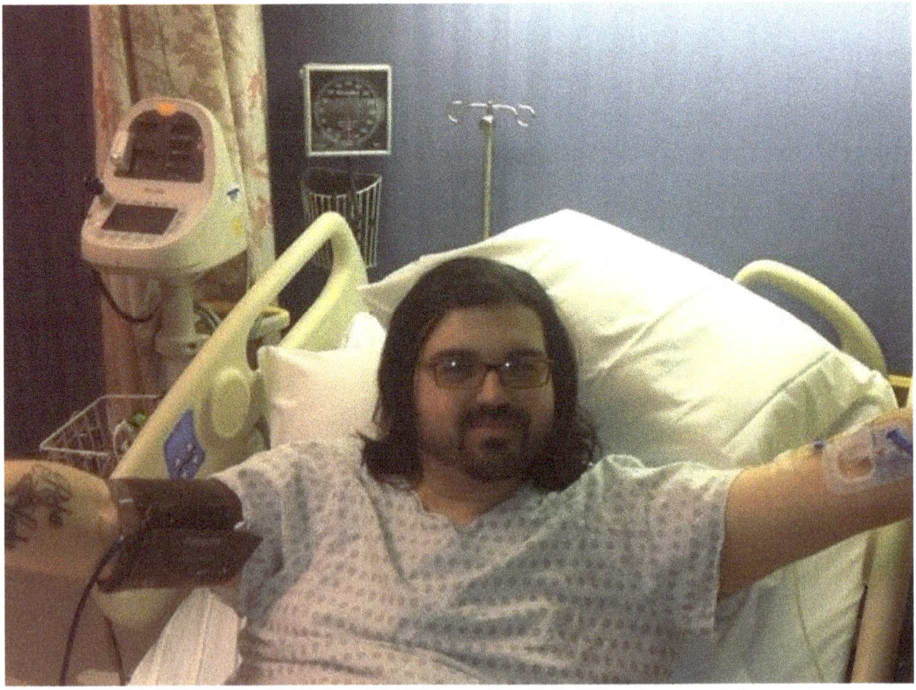

As they were preparing my transfusion, my boss, Paul, said, "Shouldn't you be more freaked out? You're kind of dying." I was in total peace. Lynn took this photo and captured that.

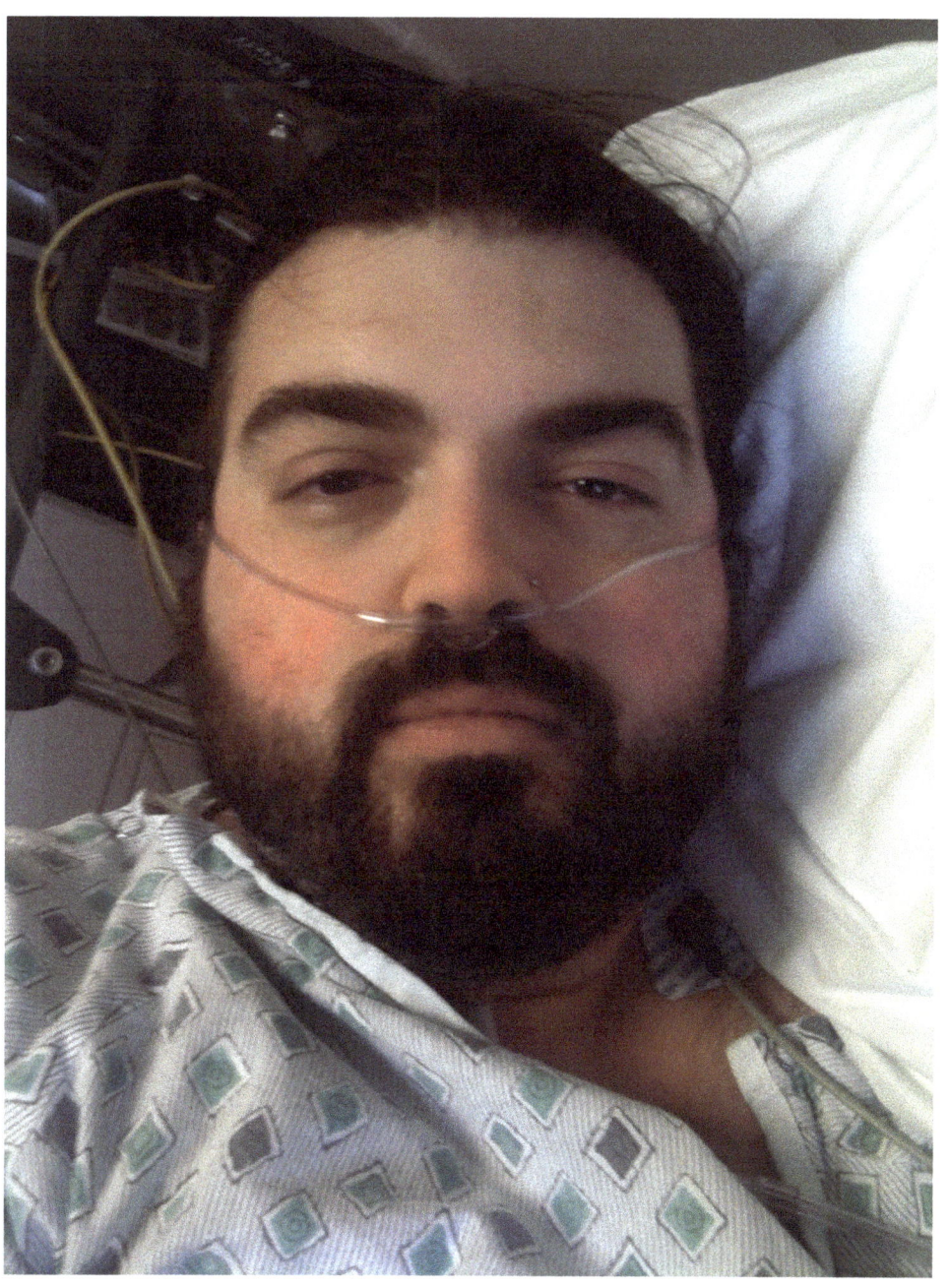

"you've studied us...you loved us
you've been our witness.
you've grieved us—we know that"

but—
there's always a but

"the only way we can live on
is if you share what we gave you...
share that thing you saw in us that made you want to do what you do
you have to plant those seeds in the world

since you decided to stay, you have to do your work
you can't stay and not do it
that's how you got in this mess that landed you in the hospital
do you understand?"

i nodded.

i opened my eyes, my face was wet
i felt my dear neighbor debbie doing reiki at my feet
the healer woman was working around my head
i felt the strength i had been lacking: strength that only comes from vision

"you're going home to do your work
where is home to you?"
nashville, i responded
"the way will be made," she declared

In 2009, I went to meet a friend for lunch at the Motown offices in Manhattan and as I walked into his office, this box of master tapes being returned to a warehouse in Nashville was the first thing I saw. This coincidence was my first indicator that I would, indeed, be going home.

RECOVERY REALIZATIONS

1/12/2012

It's been a week since my experience began in the hospital. I'm on my fourth day back at home and realizing how much freedom I have given away through the years. I've done it through putting other needs ahead of my own, through not believing that I was capable of having what I really wanted, or being afraid to verbalize the word NO when I really wanted to say it. I even convinced myself many years ago that I wanted a dream that was someone else's, not mine.

It's amazing to have been at the river and to have had no anxiety or fear of death, but I sit here today, fully facing how much anxiety and fear I have handled on a daily basis for so many years without even being conscious of it. Today, I feel it in full force and recognize it for what it is. The gift of this whole process has been this. To be able to finally see it, face it and make new decisions is a precious opportunity that I will not miss. It forces me to make those perceived "hard" decisions that are actually not choices; they are the only obvious next steps.

High Valley, January 2012
photo by Matt Muller

FREEDOM RIDE: A YEAR LATER
1/15/2012

A year ago today on MLK's birthday, I drove a ten-foot truck stuffed with my belongings and little Moja Mae and drove three hours from Queens to Clinton Corners, NY, to begin a new chapter of my life. It felt like a freedom ride in so many ways. Freedom from the things that had driven my entire life that were no longer serving me. Freedom from decisions that had backed me into a corner, into one particular way of being, that was not my core, authentic me. I knew I was coming here to heal.

It started as soon as I got here. Immediately. And I am still healing.

People want to write lots of flowery things about "healing journeys" that, quite seriously, make me want to vomit most of the time. Healing is not flowery. At least not for me. That doesn't mean that at its core it isn't beautiful, but choosing to embark on a healing path is not a matter of quoting an affirmation and waving a magic wand. It's digging your feet in and doing the work. It requires a yes and it requires follow through. It is multilayered. The safer you feel in the surrender, the deeper the work can go, and soon, that core manifests.

So, a year later, I sit in my home that I cherish, on land that speaks to me, feeds me and comforts me, as I rebirth in real time. I don't recognize myself most of the time. But that's the glory of transformation.

THE ROAD HOME
1/29/2012

it's been a beautiful sunday
it is the first entirely pain-free day i've had in quite some time
i am grateful for the painkiller (lol)
it is nice to have a day that i can be clear with my thoughts

everything about most of my physical life is in limbo
and there's something freeing about that
everything is in the air, so it's impossible for me to have answers
it is the first time, ever, that my body is a priority

my loved ones (and animals) are taking care of me
(receiving unconditional love in daily practice: another new lesson)
but, first and foremost, i am taking care of me: without apology
it is a new feeling
"no" and "i'm not up to that" are like new words to me, but i'm saying them

the blessing of experiencing pain has been incredible
learning to listen to it and hear what it is saying
how to communicate with it and feeling what it really is
not resisting, but integrating it and honoring it

what gifts james cleveland and aretha franklin have been
(i compare them to chicken noodle soup)
artists i've always loved, but never had such deep communion with
perhaps because they had/have such a grasp on the reality of life and faith
their music honors the wealth of our emotional and spiritual paths, without apology

as i can, i'm reading about death and rebirth
the emotional and spiritual roots of the physical things i am walking through
i am so assured it is right and good: it's for my growing
everything that felt dead inside is gestating and stirring (these dry bones can live!)

i am on the road home

HOLY SPIRIT
2/1/2012

there's nothing like holy spirit
a mighty rushing wind
and not in the cliche way
that's really what s/he feels like

s/he blew in today
like the most unexpected, rippling wave
with a whiff of my favorite perfume
there's no mistaking him/her

the tears came like a breaking dam
from out of my innermost being
water rushing over stones
a geyser that could not be contained

joy became tangible, palpable
more than an emotion, or state of mind
as if it became a physical being
that i had reacquainted with after years of separation

my tears merged with laughter
i let them fall as i basked in the presence
my belly shook as my soul witnessed
this mystery that i know so well

"that's holy spirit," i said.

Brigid at High Valley
designed by Johanne Renbeck (1942-2013)

3/17/2012

FLASHFORWARD

i've spent the past two days
watching the series "flashforward"

the premise is that the world experienced a blackout
two minutes and some odd seconds
each person saw months into their future and received a prophesy of sorts
it sets in motion a chain of events that forces the world to wonder
if what they saw is really destiny or if it actualizes from the mere suggestion
it reminded me of what i've always believed
as far back as the first time i heard *the prodigal…according to reba*
there has been a course, a path
something felt and intricately known inside

i have always known when i've gone off course
somehow i've always wound my way back
i recall being in the midst of heartbreak
and having a vision of five different courses i could take
and knowing the one that was "true"
but i chose another

the alternate course had no color…it was gray
and it took forever to find the road that could lead me back

when i drove home in october, i remember knowing it was time to go back
i had a flash forward of my own:
the life i dreamed of in nashville the first time around
i got offered a promotion here in new york and i let my timing get confused
or maybe the timing was exactly what it was supposed to be
i decided to stay

and then my body shut down
i heard the message: *what you are about to experience is going to take you home*
another flash forward

i saw myself crossing the state line, i saw my loved ones
i breathed in the nashville air that has its own fragrance
and i settled into my bed rest and chose to ride the rhythm

and without fail, the rhythm has begun to take me home
reevaluation of what i want, who i am, what i can and cannot do
doors have closed and other doors are opening
the timing is all its own; my job is to fall in line
then my lord will carry me home

ready or not here i come

2/21/2012

ASSIGNMENT

where have i been?

in the valley of the shadow of death
(in)decision
should i stay? should i go?
perhaps my purpose has been fulfilled
i don't know where to go next or what to do
i don't have the energy to sing
i'm tired of being in my body
every step feels too heavy
every thought too heavy
everything i loved about being here is leaving
it feels too lonely
the world has changed too much
and i don't know how to be here
somewhere i chose to stay
i was reminded of my yes
told that the yes was going to bring me home
my choice was made
the guides told me that i could have left with no judgment
but that they were glad i stayed
that i had been their witness
and had not yet truly passed on what i had gleaned from them

where am i?

in a chamber
in the process of rebirth
there are lots of tears, sleepiness, dry skin, and pains
the anxiety in comparison with "where i was" is light
but i am tuning in on the lighter anxiety in a keener way
becoming more conscious of it as my body lets go more
i can feel it with more sensitivity

and the deeper in i go, i realize this is a more innate anxiety than the fiery surface anxiety
which makes it harder to get rid of but i am learning how
i am learning to be formless in this space
to be without definition—which is a stripping away
the part of death that is still in process
i'm clear that the physical pain comes when i have reached a full emotional space
the pain allows my body to process what it has taken in emotionally
and time to process what i have absorbed through my study
--as it essentially stops me from taking in new information
in recent days, i've physically felt and seen myself in the chamber
it is a beautiful space, sparse and clean
it is silent
i feel my physical body let go, my arms go limp, my legs get warm, and i drift off
it's like being carried, but not
in that space the questions are far away
the worries that tell me i have to know what's happening next
i am rebirthing

where am i going?

i know that i am going home
that is all.

This was an assignment the 'healer woman' gave me after one of our sessions. My task was to answer the questions with no thought, with no meditation, to see what my intuitive responses were.

7/26/2012

NEW BEGINNINGS

it's hard to believe I just got out of bed in may
here I sit in los angeles
at the end of two rigorous days in the studio
creating the music I've always dreamed of making

when b called me last month about coming here and doing this*
my first thought was *"i haven't sung in almost two years.
i don't know if i can."*
but the voice inside said *"if you weren't ready, he wouldn't be calling, so go."*
and i'm so glad i did

so many messages confirming this step
the james cleveland sample being the centerpiece of this song
after i've spent the past five months absorbing his catalog...
the hook idea centering around legacy
allowing me the opportunity to write the lyric
about the dream i had in the hospital...

the experience of recording the lead vocal
is something i will never forget
b hit record for me to do a run-through
and i think we both knew during the second verse
that this was *the* take...

i felt that thing in my back
that so often comes along with the presence of the holy ghost
the cloud of witnesses was with us
b's dad, dorothy love coates, ruth davis, rev. cleveland
marion williams, teena marie, walter hawkins, albertina walker
present. stirring. moving.

---

*"b" is B. Slade, a Grammy-nominated, Dove and Stellar Award-winning singer/songwriter/producer. When we first met he was a renowned Gospel artist, recording under the moniker of Tonéx. We met shortly after I came out in 2007. He made foundation-shifting waves when he came out on Christian television in 2009.

when i hit the last note, it was as if i was suddenly unplugged
brought back to earth
i stood in one spot, uncertain of how to walk
or even if i should move
certainly i was on holy ground

the tears in b's eyes
will always be my most precious memory of this night
they fell the entire time he mixed
looking like a cross-blend of the mad scientist and a vulnerable child
i held myself, wanting to remember and never forget this:
the perfect feeling

this is the song of my life
my signpost, my center…my story
the song i will sing until i die
it is the one thing i am certain of

in the studio with B. Slade, writing and recording "The Baton"
photos by B. Slade

THE BATON
Lyrics by Tim Dillinger & B. Slade
Music by B. Slade & James Cleveland

Been running this race
Every step has made me strong
Seen roads dark and dusty
But I've been in the storm too long
Sung so many songs
And I've lived between the lines
You've been my witness
But it's finally your time

I have been kept
Day by day
I've paid the price
And I've helped to pave the way
There's always a light
That will carry you through the dark
You know there's a prize
But you've gotta press towards the mark

You've all grown up
And I must be moving on
The promised land is calling
So I'm passing the baton
I'm right behind you
Slow down, reach back, grab on
I've reached the Jordan's crossing
So I'm passing the baton

When my feet get cold, eyes shut
Body been chilled by the hand of death
Tongue glued to the roof of my mouth
My hands have been folded across my chest
Get away Jordan, get away
I've gotta cross over; it's time for me to go
Carry on, carry on
Sing your song and dance your dance
Don't forget where you came from
The bridge that brought you over
Is the one that's gonna carry you home
Keep on running, keep on pressing
I've gotta go away from here
It's time for me to go on home
I can see the gates…I can almost see them
There's twelve gates to the city
I've gotta go….I've gotta go
I won't be back no more

4/2/2014

♕ Now

That first week of January of 2012 that opens this book changed my life. What began as a diagnosis of fibromyalgia and a prescription of neurontin in the week prior brought me to a five-month medical odyssey that forever changed my course. I dealt with an acute case of idiopathic thrombocytopenic purpura, and had to take 100 mgs of prednisone for almost four months, which exacerbated every possible symptom of fibromyalgia. The ultimate diagnosis was that the ITP had been caused by chemical sensitivity—the result of bug bombing my house in the summer of 2011. Ultimately, I know that it was Spirit's way of bringing me to the river to make my choice. To live or die. To do my work...or not.

I returned to Nashville in June of 2012. Within weeks, through a series of divinely orchestrated steps, I began work on a new album with Grammy-nominated artist/ producer B. Slade. The first result of our work, a song called "The Baton," put me back on the road, and by the end of the year, I'd driven over 6,700 miles taking this message to whoever would listen. After my time of exile in upstate New York, seeing the landscape of this country was freeing. I drove relentlessly with my little Yorkie, performing and recording, bringing the vision that I had for this new music and message to life.

The result was *The Baton: 1985*, which released on June 18, 2013, the week of Juneteenth, a holiday that commemorates the announcement of the abolition of slavery. The album was a tribute to the teachers in my life, those spirits whose lives touched mine and so many others. My journey of making the album took me across the Ohio, Tennessee, and Mississippi Rivers. I will never forget them. My job is to remember. To believe.

I am back on my adventure. I left Nashville the day that I finished mixing *The Baton: 1985* and moved to Charlotte, for another assignment—remembering. I completed that season and have just moved back to New York's Hudson Valley. I'm beginning preproduction work on my next album, tentatively titled *Mystic*. My pen is full of ink. My voice has a song to sing. My mind is still curious. My heart is full of love.

I. Am. Alive.

photo by Matt Muller

7/2/2013

A Review of *The Baton: 1985*

L. Michael Gipson
SoulTracks.com

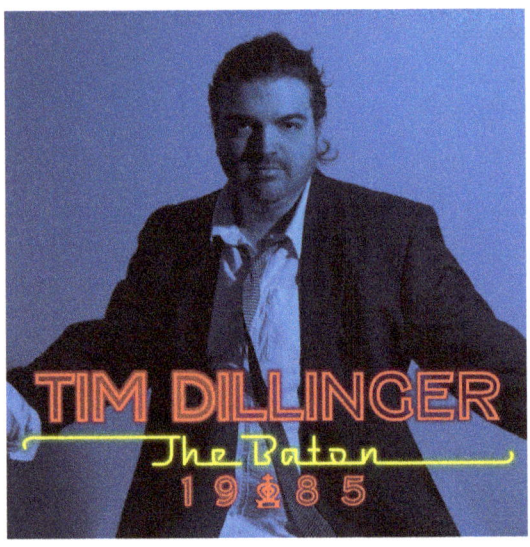

The year 1985 was musically a very transformative time in the Contemporary Gospel and Christian genres. For more than a decade, gospel was steadily marching further away from the purist, staid hymns and spirituals that marked much of the pre-1970s gospel. As with each successive generation since the days of Thomas Dorsey, acts like Commissioned, The Clark Sisters, The Winans, Andraé Crouch, The Hawkins Family, and even Amy Grant were incorporating more contemporary "secular" musical elements intended to reach a younger audience unmoved by the old-fashioned gospel music of the past but whose souls were still in need of "saving for Jesus." By 1985 a lot of these younger, dynamic, and commercially successful musical leaders were met with praise by progressives and criticism from the conservatives of the Protestant Christian world, but their sound eventually became the old guard as each new generation grow up listening to it as their "parents' gospel." Now, nearly thirty years later, there is a new crop of musicians who are not only moving the music forward, but are also pushing the socio-political boundaries of the theological world too by demanding to be heard as openly gay Christian artists who openly worship and musically bring souls to God too. Tim Dillinger is such an artist and *The Baton: 1985* is such an album.

Following several years "20 feet from the stardom" of Daryl Coley, Táta Vega and Reba Rambo-McGuire, the Nashville refined Tim Dillinger has been making boundary-pushing music almost from the beginning of his solo career. The former background singer's 2004 debut album, *Love Is On My Mind*, and most recent EP, 2011's *Gospel*, were more traditional contemporary gospel fare, but 2006's *The Muse* found Dillinger professionally out of the closet as a gay musician and playing more of the role of blue-eyed soul artist, introducing secular material not out of place on the urban adult contemporary radio dial. Part retro '80s new wave and pop rock, part modern day R&B flavored gospel, *The Baton: 1985* is unlike anything Dillinger has done before. As with other releases, Dillinger's sexuality isn't the thematic focus, praise and worship is, and yet it's a project whose theological messages are clearly liberation theory centered and inclusive in nature. Dillinger's musical activism is quieter than say his bolder, brassier contemporary, B. Slade (formerly known as Tonéx and Ton3x), but present. Throughout *The Baton: 1985*, there is a cynical eye cast toward religious dogma over God-centered relationship.

One of Dillinger's activism tells comes in the choice of the uber-controversial—and just as talented as he is whispered about—B. Slade as the producer of several cuts, including singles "The Baton" and "Say Thank You." Dillinger and Slade write both cuts, and in both cuts' sample selections find bridges to more established artists like Rev. James Cleveland and Arrested Development (B. Slade's remix version of the song includes smart interpolations of "Tennessee"). Dedicated to such gospel luminaries as Ruth Davis, Tramaine Hawkins, and Dorothy Love Coates, Dillinger establishes further ties to previous gospel trailblazers, as he—like them—creates bumping R&B music who but for the inspirational lyrics would be completely indistinguishable from the secular jams of both this era and the 80s era *The Baton: 1985* references throughout. Both jams are as uncommon and funky as their producer and as heartfelt in their messages' earnest devotion to Christ as its singer.

With the reminiscing "(Go Back To) The Old Time Way" Dillinger and co-producer Circa94 Beats digitally wash the old school gospel of yore and complicate it further with layers of New Orleans swing, rhythmic claps, Pentecostal organ play, clean hip hop and party R&B. Featuring Steffin Pfifer, "(Go Back To) The Old Time Way" also slyly makes its points both lyrically and musically of church hypocrisy, capturing the ecstasy of a "rocked" church on a spiritual high but also sly demonstrating how thin the line is from that often judging church and the high of a hood block party or bangin' club in an ecstasy of its own. The Leslie Phillips-penned "Carry You," featuring Kyla Jade, Pam Mark Hall & Patsy Moore and produced by Dillinger and Darnell Miller, does its own complication of "Wade in the Water" by lacing swamp blues, country baked banjo and bass guitar, and harmonic arrangements that echo both the Negro spiritual and contemporary electrosoul. Sinewy, fluid, and as defiant as a river, the Assata Shakur dedicated "Carry You" is a high watermark on an album that is all levee breaks.

Straight-ahead old school, Reagan-era gospel does elbow its way through the more show-off compositions. Taking a page from Andraé Crouch, co-producer Circa94 Beats infuses Jackson 5 pep into "Rain," a throwback gospel jamboree. The light funk of co-producer Eddy J Free's "More Like Jesus" could have come right out of the Al Hudson & One Way studio, with Dillinger channeling Walter Hawkins on vocals that effortlessly flow between an easy tenor and a steeple shattering falsetto. For "One," Dillinger returns to the kind of traditional Nashville material privileging 2011's *Gospel*, joined by a sage Reba Rambo-McGuire on a string flushed classical piano ballad that producer Dony McGuire arranges just a hair's breath away from the sentimental emotionalism of Joe Cocker and Jennifer Warnes' "Up Where We Belong." Each well-executed cut works in diversifying the project and highlighting the sound variances coming out of the "Born in the USA" years.

Distinguishing themselves from the rest of the material, there are two soft rock curiosities on *The Baton: 1985*. Both harken back to the Christian Contemporary music's early embrace of rock and new wave, signaling its departure and continued segregation from Black-identified gospel music as its own genre. "Threshing Floor" sports a purposefully kitschy background vocal that snitches on the track's *Back to the Future* timeline, almost as much as the synthesizer *Rocky*-like anthem on "1985" squeals on its own cinematic novelty—one whose origins could be tracked to soundtracks of B-films only available on Betamax. On both songs, Dillinger does his best Steve Winwood by way of Robert Palmer impression, nailing the role of the big haired, soulful rocker while still singing about a faith in one God for all God's children.

"I've had so many heroes, so many lives that I admired," Dillinger sings on "More Like Jesus." In too many ways to count, this album pays homage to many of those gospel heroes and sheroes who demanded an expansion of gospel to include them, their styles, and more progressive message than each previous generation. For an industry and system that has had gay, lesbian and bisexual performers since before the days of Sister Rosetta Tharpe, but preferred them silent in all matters but song, it remains to be seen whether gospel will ever stretch open enough to include those who live their lives more honestly in their walk and message. What is clear is that in talent, creativity, and musical ministries devotion to the Christian message of Christ love for everyone, artists like Dillinger and B. Slade can go toe-to-toe with the best of those conservative circles who'd leave them on the outside looking in on a house whose glass seems to grow shakier and more fragile by the year. In the meantime, pioneering projects like *The Baton: 1985* continue to find inspiration in the firebrands of gospel's soulful past while still trying to blaze a new trail as part of the music and the church's potentially more inclusive future.

♛ ACKNOWLEDGMENTS

Moja Mae—Can a dog be a soulmate? I think so. Thank you for the healing work that we have done together. *"You touched me...you changed me..."*

Harpo, Miss Sophia, Shug, Celie and Nettie (my High Valley kittens)—I think of you every day and miss you tremendously. The love that we exchanged cannot be put into words. I hope you know how much you mean to me.

Debbie—Thank you for your care during my illness and for joining your life with ours in this new chapter in the Hudson Valley. What a joy!

Des—What a chapter we've written together, Sis. I'm so proud of you. Eternally connected and always cheering you on! We've got your slippers warming by the fire.

Matt—I never could have imagined the collaboration that would spring from our first meeting. Thank you for documenting my death and rebirth in photographic form these past three years--a gift I can never repay.

To my family—in blood and in spirit—who all came to my aid when I was ill and helped me make the necessary transitions to come back to life.

Maeve, Elizabeth and Douglas—To say you have been essential would be an understatement. Thank you for providing the healing space in both a literal and figurative sense. *What a fellowship, what a joy divine.* I'll meet you at the Falls!

Lynn—When I met you, I knew we were family. What changes we have been through together! Thank you for the gift of your love and Whaley Lake. You both carry such magic.

Marion—Who knew the day we met, sitting on the swings at High Valley, that life would take us on this road! Abu Dhabi, Nashville, Charlotte and everywhere in between. Here we are. You have my eternal gratitude.

David—Through many dangers, toils and snares...and side-eyes! What we share is rich and sacred. We've been a witness for each other and that means the world. Heaven!!!

Mickey Boyce-Ellis—You will never know how much the time we spent together during my visits to Los Angeles meant to me. Your strength, wit and wisdom inspire me. *"365. That's how much I love you dear..."*

Ray, my husband—Last, but certainly not least. Your love has transformed me. Thank you for dreaming with me. Your patience and creativity made this book a reality. Together, we are unstoppable. I love you. *"You make me feel at last I belong..."*

www.ingramcontent.com/pod-product-compliance
Lightning Source LLC
Chambersburg PA
CBHW040416100526
44588CB00022B/2849